GERM INVADERS
YOUR AMAZING IMMUNE SYSTEM

MEGAN BORGERT-SPANIOL

Big Buddy Books

An Imprint of Abdo Publishing
abdobooks.com

abdobooks.com

Published by Abdo Publishing, a division of ABDO, PO Box 398166, Minneapolis, Minnesota 55439. Copyright © 2021 by Abdo Consulting Group, Inc. International copyrights reserved in all countries. No part of this book may be reproduced in any form without written permission from the publisher. Big Buddy Books™ is a trademark and logo of Abdo Publishing.

Printed in the United States of America, North Mankato, Minnesota
102020
012021

Design: Sarah DeYoung, Mighty Media, Inc.
Production: Mighty Media, Inc.
Editor: Rebecca Felix

Cover Photographs: Shutterstock (all)
Interior Photographs: Shutterstock (all)
Design Elements: Shutterstock (all)

Library of Congress Control Number: 2020940284

Publisher's Cataloging-in-Publication Data
Names: Borgert-Spaniol, Megan, author.
Title: Your amazing immune system / by Megan Borgert-Spaniol
Description: Minneapolis, Minnesota : Abdo Publishing, 2021 | Series: Germ invaders | Includes online resources and index
Identifiers: ISBN 9781532194252 (lib. bdg.) | ISBN 9781098213619 (ebook)
Subjects: LCSH: Immunity--Juvenile literature. | Immune system--Juvenile literature. | Immunopathology--Juvenile literature. | Health behavior--Juvenile literature. | Immunoglobulins--Juvenile literature.
Classification: DDC 616.079--dc23

CONTENTS

Your Amazing Body..4
When Germs Attack..6
All about the Immune System................................8
White Blood Cells...10
Antibodies..12
Immunity...14
Vaccines..16
Immune System at Work.......................................18
Immune System Disorders.................................. 20
Getting Better 22
When to See a Doctor..24
Antibiotics..26
Healthy Habits..28
Glossary 30
Online Resources 31
Index..32

YOUR AMAZING BODY

You are amazing! So is your body. Most of the time your body works just fine. But sometimes germs **invade** it. Germs can make you sick. When this happens, your immune system works to fight the **infection**.

GET TO KNOW GERMS

Germs are tiny **organisms**. They can live inside people, plants, and animals. There are four main types of germs.

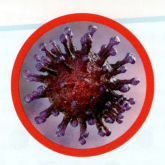

VIRUSES

Viruses are parasitic. This means they cannot survive on their own. They require a host cell to reproduce.

BACTERIA

Bacteria are single-celled creatures. They can survive on their own or inside another living organism.

PROTOZOA

Protozoa are single-celled creatures. Some can survive on their own. Others are parasitic.

FUNGI

Fungi are plant-like organisms. They get their food from people, plants, and animals.

WHEN GERMS ATTACK

When a **disease**-causing germ enters your body, you won't know it right away. But your immune system **detects** the germ! It springs into action.

INVASION

Germs enter your body through the mouth, nose, or eyes. Germs can also enter though cuts in the skin.

ATTACK

The **invading** germs begin to make copies. They spread inside your body.

ALARM

Your immune system **detects** the germs. Your body sends white blood cells to fight the **invaders**.

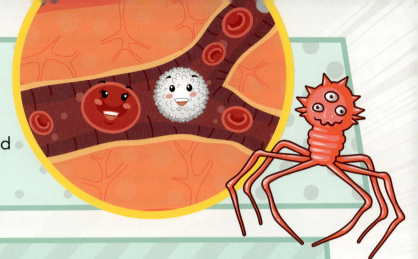

FIGHT

Some white blood cells eat the germ invaders. Other white blood cells create antibodies. Antibodies protect you from the same germ if it ever invades again.

RECOVER

Once your white blood cells have destroyed the germ invaders, you feel better! How long this takes depends on the illness.

ALL ABOUT THE IMMUNE SYSTEM

Your immune system is made up of tissues, cells, proteins, and organs. This system works to keep germs from entering your body. When germs do **invade**, the immune system fights them.

Antigens are found on the surface of germ cells. An antigen is the part of the germ the immune system **detects**. Your body sends out white blood cells to fight the antigen.

White blood cells find the antigen and attack it. This battle can make you feel sick. But the **symptoms** you feel are signs your immune system is doing its job!

Your skin is your body's first line of defense against germs. Tears and mucus also work to keep germs out.

WHITE BLOOD CELLS

White blood cells are always present in your bloodstream. But during an **infection**, your body makes more white blood cells than normal. The white blood cells help fight the infection.

There are different types of white blood cells. One type eats the germs that cause infection. Another type of white blood cells helps the body remember germs. They protect against these germs if they ever enter your body again.

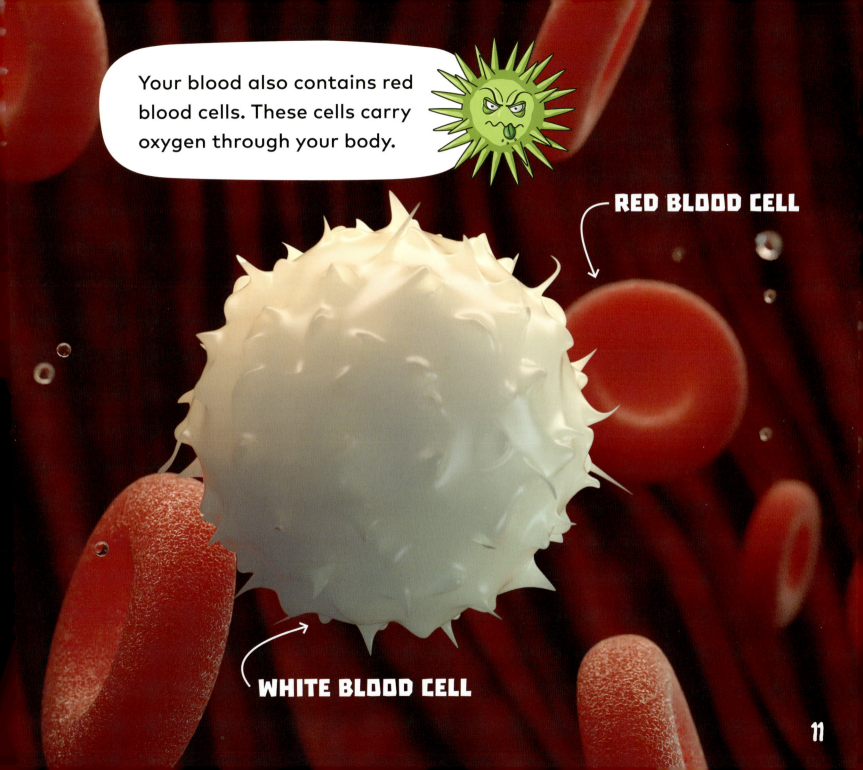

ANTIBODIES

How do white blood cells protect the body against future germs? Certain white blood cells are called B cells. These cells make antibodies.

An antibody is a special protein. Each antibody is made to attack a specific type of **antigen**. Some types of antibodies lock onto antigens. This flags the antigens so other cells know to kill it. Other types of antibodies lock onto and kill antigens.

After the antigens are destroyed, antibodies remain in your body. The antibodies will **detect** the same germ right away if it enters your body again. They will be ready to fight it.

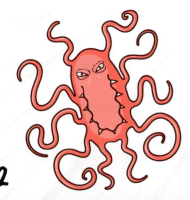

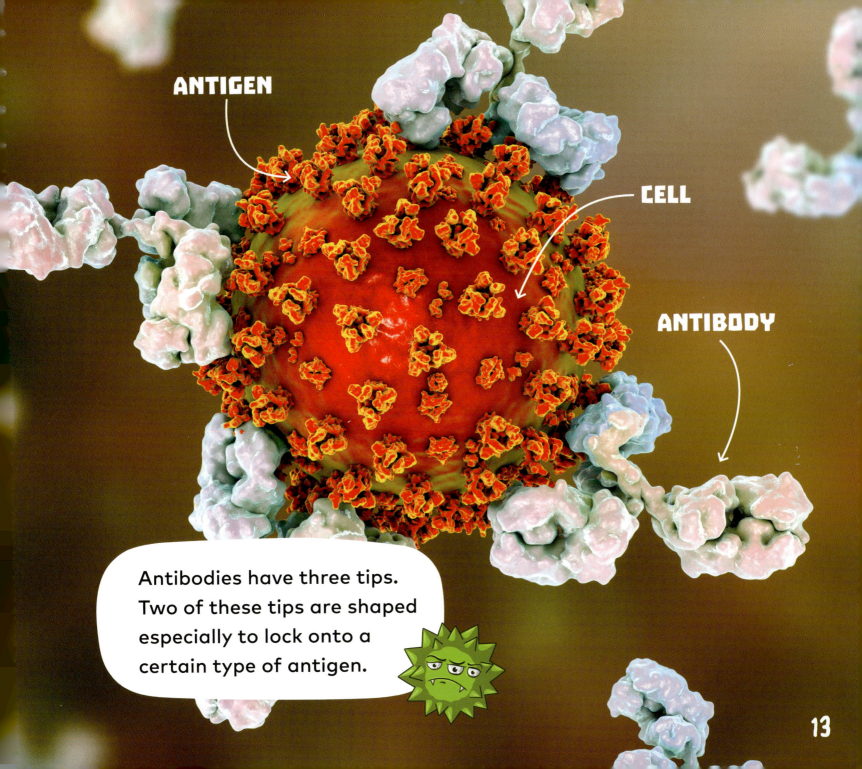

IMMUNITY

When your body has antibodies for a certain germ, you are said to be immune to that germ. Sometimes this effect can fade. But usually it lasts, making you better prepared to fight the germ if you come in contact with it again.

As we grow, we come in contact with more and more germs. So, our bodies make and store more and more antibodies. This is one reason why kids get sick more often than adults. Their immune systems are still developing!

VACCINES

Do you remember the last time you got a shot, or **vaccination**? Most young kids are vaccinated against many **diseases**.

A vaccination puts a small amount of a germ into your body. The germ in the vaccine is already dead or weakened. So, it doesn't cause an **infection**. But it still causes your body to take action!

Your immune system **detects** the germ. It creates antibodies to help protect you if you are exposed to the germ again.

SCIENCE BREAKTHROUGH

In the first half of the 1900s, many thousands of Americans got polio every year. Polio can cause **paralysis** and even death. The polio vaccine came out in the 1950s. It has kept polio from originating in the US for more than 40 years.

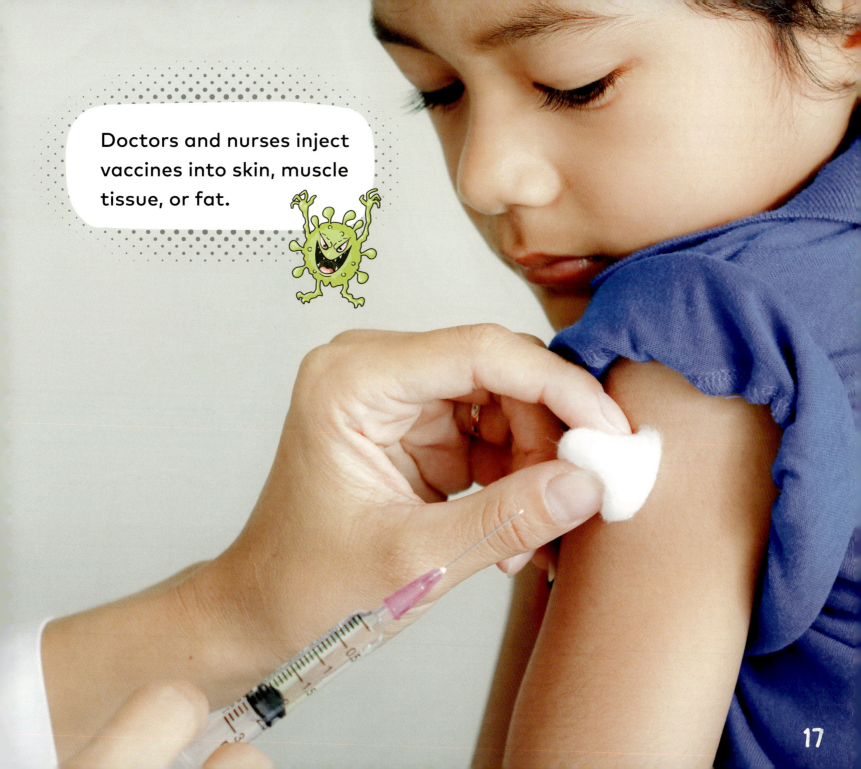

Doctors and nurses inject vaccines into skin, muscle tissue, or fat.

IMMUNE SYSTEM AT WORK

Vaccines immunize us against many illnesses. But not all illnesses have vaccines. One example is the common cold. More than 200 different virus germs cause colds. Each of these germs would need a vaccine! This is too many for scientists to create.

When a germ you are not vaccinated against **invades**, your body fights back. This fight causes **symptoms** that make you feel sick.

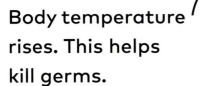

Body temperature rises. This helps kill germs.

Nasal membranes produce extra mucus. This traps germs and sends them out of the body.

Damaged cells release chemicals that cause inflammation. These chemicals also attract white blood cells to the damaged cells.

Dead white blood cells may build up into pus. This thick liquid can result from wounds, ear infections, and other causes.

19

IMMUNE SYSTEM DISORDERS

Symptoms often result from your immune system working. But sometimes, they mean more. They can signal an immune system disorder.

People can be born with weak immune systems. Or, they can get **diseases** that weaken their immune systems.

Germs are a greater risk to people with weak immune systems. These people can get seriously ill from **infections**.

Immune systems can also **overreact** to something harmless, such as pollen. This is what causes **allergic** reactions.

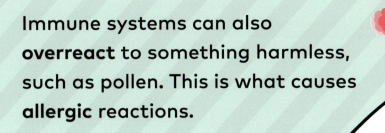

Allergic reactions range from mild to deadly.

Finally, some people have immune systems that attack their own healthy cells. This leads to **autoimmune diseases**.

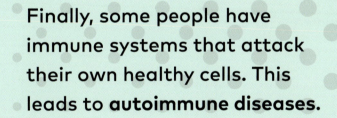

Crohn's **disease** is an autoimmune disease. It affects the **digestive system**.

GETTING BETTER

A healthy immune system can usually fight off common illnesses. But you can help it fight!

Get rest when you are sick. Rest allows your body to put its energy toward attacking germs.

It's also important to drink lots of water. This is because it's easy to get **dehydrated** when you're sick. Drinking water also helps loosen and drain extra **mucus**.

Over-the-counter medicines can help ease symptoms when you're sick. But these medicines don't cure the illness.

WHEN TO SEE A DOCTOR

Symptoms from minor **infections** usually last for about one week. But sometimes symptoms last longer or feel **severe**. In these cases, your immune system may need help. The following symptoms are signs it's time to see a doctor.

Increased swelling, redness, or **pus** around a wound

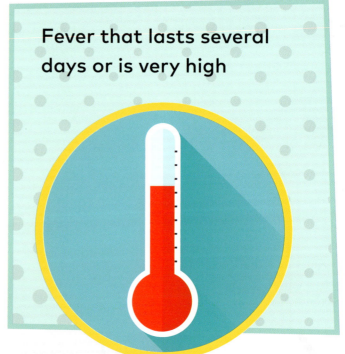

Fever that lasts several days or is very high

24

Inability to drink and eat without throwing up

Trouble breathing

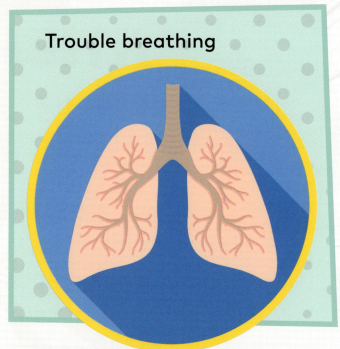

Painful cough

Severe pain (ears, throat, stomach, chest)

ANTIBIOTICS

During your visit, the doctor might suggest you take antibiotics. These drugs kill or slow the growth of bacteria. They only treat bacterial **infections**. Antibiotics won't treat viruses, such as colds.

And while antibiotics kill harmful bacteria, they can also kill good bacteria. Good bacteria help your immune system. Destroying them can increase risk of infection. Because of this, doctors must only have patients take antibiotics when necessary.

SCIENCE BREAKTHROUGH

Antibiotics were discovered in the 1920s. They were made available to consumers in the 1940s. Penicillin is an antibiotic that treats infections such as strep throat. It was first used in 1942.

STREPTOCOCCUS PYOGENES BACTERIA

Strep throat is a bacterial infection. It is caused by bacteria called *Streptococcus pyogenes*.

HEALTHY HABITS

Your immune system is amazing! It guards against and fights germs. You can help keep your immune system strong with healthy habits.

- ☐ Do relaxing activities to reduce stress. Take a walk, listen to music, or draw.
- ☐ Include a rainbow of fruits and vegetables in your daily diet.
- ☐ Get enough sleep to feel well-rested in the morning.
- ☐ Wash your hands often for at least 20 seconds with soap and water.

Infections can be dangerous. But thanks to your amazing immune system, science, and some healthy habits, your body is ready to face these germ **invaders**!

29

GLOSSARY

allergic (A-luhr-jek)—having a condition in which coming in contact with a certain thing causes coughing, sneezing, or a rash.

antigen—a substance that is foreign to the body and causes an immune system response.

autoimmune disease—a disease relating to, or caused by, cells that attack the organism producing them.

dehydrated—lacking ample fluid or water.

detect—to discover or notice.

digestive system (deye-JEHST-iv SIH-stem)—the group of organs that break down food into simpler substances the body can absorb.

disease—a sickness.

infection—a condition in which a germ has entered the body and caused disease.

invade—to enter and spread with the intent to take over. Something that does this is an invader.

mucus (MYOO-kuhs)—thick, slippery, protective fluid from the body.

organism—a living thing.

overreact—to react to something too strongly.

paralysis (puh-RA-luh-suhs)—a loss of the power to move or feel part of the body.

pus—a thick fluid that is usually yellowish-white and forms as part of an inflammatory response to an infection.

severe (suh-VIHR)—causing danger, hardship, or pain.

symptom—a noticeable change in the normal working of the body. A symptom indicates or accompanies disease, sickness, or other malfunction.

vaccine (vak-SEEN)—a substance given by shot to prevent illness or disease. Receiving this shot is called vaccination.

ONLINE RESOURCES

Booklinks
NONFICTION NETWORK
FREE! ONLINE NONFICTION RESOURCES

To learn more about the immune system, please visit **abdobooklinks.com** or scan this QR code. These links are routinely monitored and updated to provide the most current information available.

INDEX

allergic reactions, 21
animals, 5
antibiotics, 26
antibodies, 7, 12, 13, 14, 15, 16
antigen, 8, 12, 13
autoimmune diseases, 21

B cells, 12
bacteria, 5, 26, 27
blood, 10, 11
breathing, 25

chest, 25
colds, 18, 26
coughing, 25
Crohn's disease, 21

digestive system, 21
doctors, 17, 24, 26

ear infections, 19
ears, 25
eyes, 6

fever, 19, 24
fruits, 28

hydration, 22, 25

immune system disorders, 20, 21
immunity, 14, 18
inflammation, 19, 21, 24

mouth, 6
mucus, 9, 19, 22

nose, 6, 19
nurses, 17

over-the-counter medicines, 23
oxygen, 11

pain, 25
paralysis, 16
penicillin, 26
plants, 5, 28
polio, 16
pollen, 21
proteins, 7, 8, 12
protozoa, 5
pus, 19, 24

red blood cells, 11

scientists, 18
skin, 6, 9, 17
stomach, 25
strep throat, 26, 27
stress, 28
symptoms, 8, 18, 19, 20, 23, 24

tears, 9
throat, 25, 26
tissues, 8, 17

vaccines, 16, 17, 18
vegetables, 28
viruses, 5, 18, 26
vomiting, 25

washing hands, 28
white blood cells, 7, 8, 10, 12, 19